CORRIE'S CHRISTMAS MEMORIES

Corrie's Christmas Memories

Corrie ten Boom

Fleming H. Revell Company
Old Tappan, New Jersey

Scripture references in this volume are based on the King James Version of the Bible.

Library of Congress Cataloging in Publication Data

ten Boom, Corrie.
  Corrie's Christmas memories.

  CONTENTS: The Christmas story told by Corrie. —
A Christmas story, "Father Martin". — Casper ten
Boom's Christmas message. — Corrie's memories of Christmases past. [etc.]
  1. Christmas. [1. Christmas] I. Title.
HV45.T43   242'.33   76-17649
ISBN 0-8007-0822-9

CONTENTS

Christmas!
Christmas joy!
Jesus is born!

I want to tell you a little bit of what I remember about Christmases in my life. I am now eighty-four years old. When I think of Christmas Eves, Christmas feasts, Christmas songs, and Christmas stories, I know it was not a short and transient gladness. It was — and is — a joy unspeakable and full of glory.

God loved the world and sent His Son. Whosoever believes in Him will not perish, but have everlasting life.

That is the Christmas joy.

The Christmas joy is possible for everybody, for Jesus said, "Come to me *all*."

Betsie and I were always a team at the Christmas feasts. One told *the* Christmas story of Luke 2, the other *a* Christmas story.

CORRIE TEN BOOM

1
The Christmas Story
How I Told It

Joseph was very concerned. You could see it in his face.

"What's the matter, Joseph?" Mary asked.

"We have to go to Bethlehem. Everyone has to be registered in the place where their ancestors lived. We are David's descendants, so we have to go to the city of David, Bethlehem. Oh, Mary! Now we must travel when you are about to give birth to a child . . . Mary, you do not look concerned at all!"

"Joseph, I have not told you yet that I have had to struggle with a problem. Our child is not *our* child only. He is the Messiah and the prophets have told that Christ the Messiah — the Lord — will be born in Bethlehem and not in Nazareth where we live. Oh, Joseph, now we are going to Bethlehem and God has really shown that our times are in His hands. He never makes a mistake."

It was a rather big company which left from Nazareth for the same purpose as Joseph and Mary, but later the same day the others went ahead as quickly as possible in order to reach Bethlehem early. Joseph and Mary were left alone. Joseph carefully led the donkey on which Mary was sitting over the roughly paved way. But then at last they saw Bethlehem from the top of a mountain. The setting sun shone on the flat roofs of Bethlehem's houses. When they passed the fields near the little town, shepherds were watching over the sheep. Joseph greeted them.

"Good evening, shepherds! Have you had a good day? . . . Can you tell me the way to an inn?"

"Rather busy. Crowds of people have been passing our fields all day. More than ever before. The sheep were unruly. They are not used to that! The inn? It's there near the beginning of the street, then a little bit to the right."

"Thanks."

The innkeeper was standing at the gate of the inn. He looked at Mary. "Sorry we have no room for you. All day streams of guests have entered

Bethlehem. We do not have a large inn. The house is filled to the brim."

"Have you not one corner where my wife can sleep? She is expecting her baby soon."

"I see. . . . Wait!" said the innkeeper. "Go around the house where there's a stable. Perhaps there is a corner there."

As Joseph went to see if there was a place, he told Mary, "Wait here. God will show me where I can find room for this night."

Now Mary was alone; she looked around. It was quiet and dark in the streets, for there were no street lamps and the windows were in the rear of the houses.

"Lord, You know that our child is coming soon," Mary whispered. She felt great peace in her heart.

At last she saw Joseph coming around the corner.

"I have found something for you and the donkey and . . . the baby." He led the donkey around till they came to the back of the inn. Joseph showed how he had placed some clean straw on

11

the floor for Mary in a corner of the stable.

"Look what I have for the baby!" He pulled a manger from the other side. Joseph had cleaned it and put some fresh straw in it. It was really like a little bed.

"Now you try to sleep a bit, Mary. I will watch." Joseph went to the door of the stable and looked through the night over the now-dark fields. He heard angry voices coming from the inn.

"What a time we live in!" a harsh voice was shouting. "Terrible to have to obey that dictator! How long will it last? I had to leave my business to be registered here."

A soft voice said, "The Messiah will liberate us . . . the prophets . . . ."

Loud voices — all at the same time — interrupted her words. Joseph could not hear the rest of what she said. He looked at the scene before him. It was a bright moonless night. Stars — so many stars — were shining. He saw sheep with the shepherds who kept watch over them.

At last the voices in the inn stopped, and then

everything was quiet, silent, nothing moved.

And in that silent night, Jesus was born.

Mary had swaddling clothes in the bundle she had packed. (At that time mothers never made baby clothing before the birth of a child.) Mary wrapped the little baby up to the tiny arms, then one little leg, then the other little leg. Then the whole little body. Then she laid Him in the manger and tucked Him in with the rest of the swaddling clothes.

"Now try to sleep, Mary. I will watch," Joseph said. He leaned against the door frame and looked over the fields.

But Mary spoke softly, "Joseph, our baby is not our baby only. He is the baby of the world . . . but nobody knows it. Only we."

Then she fell asleep. Joseph watched. Suddenly he heard footsteps coming around the inn, straight to the stable. Men's footsteps.

It is good that I watch, Joseph thought. He stood now so that nobody could pass by him into the stable.

"Excuse us," an old man said. "We want to

look in the stable."

"Sorry, not now," Joseph replied.

"Please, let us only look in the manger."

"No," said Joseph firmly, "especially not in the manger, for there lies a just-born baby."

"It is for the baby we came!"

Joseph suddenly heard Mary's voice.

"Joseph! Let them in! Come, folks, and tell me how you know about the baby. Come in, men." Joseph stood aside. The men entered the stable. There Mary saw all the men and a few boys kneeling before the baby.

For a moment it was quiet. Everyone felt the silent night. But then one of the men started to speak:

"We were watching over the sheep and talking about what had happened during the day. Never had so many people passed over the fields. All came to be registered. David is the ancestor to many . . . . I said: *When will there ever be an end to this horrible dictatorship! No freedom. Roman slaves!*"

The man then pointed to the oldest shep-

herd. "He gave the answer when he said, 'It is the Messiah who will bring peace. The prophets have told us!' And he read for us what Isaiah had said about the coming King of Israel. We listened; we all believe it — yes — *and then it happened!*"

There was a silent moment. All looked at the baby Jesus.

"Yes. Then it happened," the old shepherd now continued. "Suddenly an angel stood before us. He was light and beautiful and all of us were frightened, but he said:

'Do *not* be afraid! Listen. I bring you glorious news of great joy, which is for all people. This very day, in David's town, a Saviour has been born for you. He is Christ the Lord. Let this prove it to you: *You will find a baby, wrapped up and lying in a manger — wrapped up in swaddling clothes.'*"

The shepherd was silent again. Everyone felt the holy night. The boy who was standing the closest to the baby told more of the story.

"And then we heard and saw . . . a piece of heaven! All around us were angels as light as the lightest sunshine and they sang — oh, how they sang!

> Glory to God in the highest heaven!
> Peace on earth among men of good will.

"Yes, it was as if God had opened a little corner of the veil that we could see and hear a little bit of heaven. But then . . . they were gone, and it was dark," the boy went on, "so dark . . . darker than it ever was before. After that heavenly light the earth was so dark — so terribly dark."

The old shepherd continued the story.

"Yes, and that boy said, 'Let us go and see the baby.' I asked, 'How can we find him?' The boy answered, 'Now that is easy! He is lying in the manger.' 'Yes, of course! Our manger! You are right,' I said, 'Let's go straight to Bethlehem and see this thing which the Lord has made known to us.' So we ran as fast as we could. Now you know why we came here."

"Oh, Joseph! We are not the only ones who know that the baby has been born — the baby of the whole world — but the *angels* know and the shepherds know," said Mary.

"Yes, and we will tell all those around us tomorrow," the oldest shepherd said.

All the men and boys stood up and left the stable on tiptoe — very quiet. They were so happy — so happy!

"We know it, the angels and shepherds know it, and all whom the shepherds will tell tomorrow," Mary whispered, "but what about the rest of the world — that great, wide, great, wide world for whom the child was born?"

A few days later, Joseph heard a knock on the door. (They were now in a nice place. Someone had heard from the shepherds about the baby and had given them a room for as long as they needed it.) Joseph opened the door, and there stood some very dignified people, beautifully dressed, and stately camels were standing beside them.

"May we enter?" a dark man asked. "We should like to see the baby."

Joseph stood aside and three men came in. Mary had the baby on her lap and saw with amazement the rich men kneeling reverently in front of the baby.

"The King of Israel," one of the men said. "The King of the world!"

Joseph whispered, "Tell us how you know about it."

They all sat down and one man spoke:

"We are astronomers and we are friends. We study the stars and books about the stars. When we find something we always tell each other. One night we *all three saw The Star*. We came together to talk about what star this could be. We had never seen that one before. We took our books and could not find anything until we read in a very old book about a prophet — Balaam. He was a real prophet, but a bad king hired him to curse Israel. He wanted to obey that king, but could say only what God told him. Instead of cursing Israel, Balaam blessed it, and told about a

18

king that would come — one who would bring peace. And that a Star would appear that had never been seen before (*see* Numbers 24:17). We decided to go to Israel and during the night The Star always went before us in the sky — until it shone immediately above your house."

The men opened their bundles and placed beautiful rich presents at the foot of the child Jesus. Gold, incense, and myrrh — presents which were given only to kings.

Then the Wise Men left.

"Oh, Joseph! Not only we, the shepherds, the people in Bethlehem, and the angels know — but now the people in the far, far country where the Wise Men will also now tell about Jesus. Everyone should know our baby."

May I tell you a little bit of the rest of the story?

That same night God told Joseph to take Mary and the child to Egypt because Herod the king was going to try to kill Jesus. Joseph obeyed immediately for he was used to obeying God. In the night they went away from Bethlehem — in the dark, over the fields. They greeted the shepherds who asked them how the baby was doing. Egypt was very far, but when they arrived there, I can imagine that it was not difficult for Joseph to find work. People like to have a good carpenter available. And, my, how good it was that they had the rich presents from the Wise Men — gold, incense, and myrrh. They stayed as long as necessary in Egypt, and then went back to Nazareth. You can read in the Bible much of what happened after that.

When I think of this story it makes me so happy. Do you know why? Because I know that the baby Jesus was born in Bethlehem for the whole world — also for you and me. You and I know much more than the shepherds — or even the Wise Men — knew. We know that Jesus died on the cross for the sins of the whole world — also for your sins and mine. He will give us forgiveness when we tell Him of our sins. That is possible because Jesus not only died for us — He lives! He rose from the dead and has said:

I am with you till the end of the world.

I believe it. I don't understand it, but that does not matter. For at the same time He is with you and me, He is with the Father in heaven and there He pleads for us. Is that not a joy? Jesus will come again, though not as a little baby but as a mighty King, who will make everything new.

The best is yet to come. We will see Him face-to-face.

But I won't tell you more now. Would you like to know it all? Then read the Bible!

Ruben Saillenn was a powerful French evangelist. His ministry in France at the beginning of our century resulted in thousands of Frenchmen receiving Christ. He was called the Spurgeon of France.

Saillenn was the author of the moving Christmas story "Martin, the Shoemaker." Later on, the same story appeared as one of Leo Tolstoy's writings, and Saillenn wrote to Tolstoy to clarify the matter. Tolstoy answered, and apologized for the fact that he had been wrongly credited with writing the tale, admitting that he had taken it over and adapted it from a British publication. Tolstoy's letter still exists as proof. When some of Saillenn's relatives were asked for permission to use it, they answered, "Ruben Saillenn never copyrighted the story as he did not want to limit its circulation, but he wished it to be used freely and as widely as possible."

2
<u>A</u> Christmas Story
"Father Martin"

Don't you know Father Martin? Though he is only a poor shoemaker, yet he does not live in an attic. His workshop, his living room, his bedroom, and his kitchen — they are all in one in a small, wooden building at the corner of a square and a street in the center of the old part of Marseilles in France. There he lives a philosophical life. He is neither too rich nor too poor, as he repairs the shoes of all the people in the neighborhood. For since his eyes have been growing older, the good man has not made any new shoes.

Although you do not know him, the fishermen of Quartier St. Jean and the women of the market on the square do know him — and also the urchins of the municipal school who pass his door like a swarm of bees when the church clock strikes four.

He has put patches on all their shoes; he knows where the shoes hurt them. The housewives trust only him for repairing their sons' shoes in a solid way, because the boys ruin the best shoes within a fortnight.

For some time now Father Martin has had the reputation of being pious. Not that he is afraid of the laughing, but since he has been going to the "meetings," as they are called (where hymns are sung and people speak about God), he has changed. He doesn't work less or worse. On the contrary. He is no longer seen at the café as in former days. He has a large Book which one often sees him reading when one looks through the small window. He seems far happier than before.

Father Martin has had a great deal of sorrow. His wife died more than twenty years ago; his son, a sailor, has not come home for ten years. As for his daughter — he never speaks of her. If anybody asks him what has become of her, a shadow passes over his face and instead of answering, he just bows his head.

But then — even in the days when he went to the café after his daily work for a game of cards with his comrades — the old shoemaker was rarely really happy. At present, as we have said, he seems to be happier; his large Book is apparently the cause of this.

It was Christmas Eve. Outside it was cold and wet, but in Father Martin's dwelling it was light and warm. He had finished his work and had eaten his soup. His small stove was roaring and he sat in a wicker chair, his eyeglasses on his nose, reading: "Because there was no room for them in the inn" (Luke 2:7).

Here the reader stopped to ponder. "No room," he said, "no room for *Him!*"

He looked at his room, small and clean, though poor. "There would have been room for Him here," he added, "if He had come. What happiness to receive Him! I would have felt ashamed and would no doubt have left the whole place to Him! . . . No room for Him! Oh, why doesn't He come and ask me for room . . . ?

"I am alone; I have no one to think of. Everybody has his relatives and friends. Who on earth cares for me? I would love Him to keep me company!

"If today had been the first Christmas? If tonight the Saviour would come to the earth? If He would choose to enter my small house? How I would look after Him! How I would worship Him! Why does He not reveal Himself today as He did formerly?

"What might I give to Him? The Bible tells what the Wise Men offered: gold, frankincense, myrrh; I have nothing of all that; these Wise Men were rich. But the shepherds — what did they give to Him? It does not say. Perhaps they had no time to take anything with them . . . . Ah! I know what I would give to Him!"

He got up and reached out toward a shelf on which there were two tiny shoes, carefully wrapped up. Two baby shoes.

"Look," he said, "this is what I would have given to Him — my masterpiece. The mother would love it! But what am I thinking of?" he added smiling to himself. "Really, I am talking nonsense. How can I imagine such things? As if my Saviour had need of my little home and my shoes!"

The old man sat down again and continued his thinking. More and more people appeared in the streets as the evening passed. The sound of people going to Christmas dinners was heard. But Father Martin did not move; he had probably fallen asleep.

"Martin," a soft voice said quite close to him.

"Who is there?" the shoemaker called out, suddenly awake. But it was no use looking at the door; he did not see anybody.

"Martin, you wanted to see Me. Well, look into the street — tomorrow — from morning till night; you will see Me pass at some time. Try to recognize Me — for I shall not show Myself to you again."

The voice was silent; Martin rubbed his eyes. His lamp had gone out for lack of paraffin oil. All the clocks struck midnight: Christmas had come.

"It is He," the old man said. "He promised to pass my house! But perhaps it was a dream? That does not matter! I shall await Him. I have never seen Him, but did I not admire His picture in all the churches? I shall no doubt recognize Him."

Then Martin went to bed, and for quite a while the strange words he had heard occupied his thoughts.

Long before daybreak the shoemaker's little lamp was lit. He put more coals into his stove (which had not yet burned out) and started making his coffee. He then quickly tidied his room and sat down near the window to await the first daylight and the first passersby.

Gradually the sky became brighter, and Martin saw the road sweeper on the square — the first of all men to appear. He gave him only a swift look; he surely had other things to do than to watch a sweeper!

But it seemed to be cold outside, for the glass was all the time covered with vapor, and the man — after some vigorous sweeps — started a more energetic movement to get warm by beating his arms around his body and stamping his feet.

"The poor man," Martin said, "he still is cold. It is a feast day today — but not for him. What about offering him a cup of coffee?" And he knocked against the window.

The sweeper turned his head, saw Father Martin behind his window, and came near. The shoemaker opened his door. "Come in," he said, "warm yourself."

"I won't say *no* to that, thank you. What beastly weather! One would think one was in Russia."

"Would you like a cup of coffee?" Father Martin asked.

"Well, you are a good man! With pleasure, of course. Better late than never to have a little Christmas meal."

The shoemaker quickly served his guest and then hastened back to his window, searching the street and square on all sides to see whether anybody had passed.

"What are you looking at outside?" the sweeper asked at last.

"I am expecting my Master," Martin answered.

"Your Master? So you work at a factory. What a time to visit your workmen! Today is a feast for you!"

"I am speaking of another Master," the old shoemaker said.

"Oh!"

"A Master who can arrive at any moment and who promised me to come today. You won't know His name; it is Jesus."

"I have heard people talk about Him, but I don't know Him. Where does He live?"

Then in a few words Father Martin told the sweeper the story he read the night before, adding a few details. While he talked he turned to the window.

"And do you expect Him?" the workman said at last when he knew who was meant. "I have an idea you won't see Him the way you think. But it does not matter; you have shown Him to me. Will you let me borrow your Book, Mister . . . ?"

"Martin," the shoemaker said.

"Mr. Martin, I assure you, you have not wasted your time this morning, though the day has hardly begun. Thank you and good-bye!"

Then the workman went away, leaving Father Martin alone once more, his face close to the

window.

Later a few drunkards passed by; the old shoe-maker did not even look at them. Then the street vendors arrived with their small wagons. He knew them too well to take much notice of them.

But after one or two hours his eyes were drawn towards a young woman, miserably dressed, with a child in her arms. She was so pale, so thin, that it touched the old man's heart. Perhaps she caused him to think of his own daughter. He opened his door and called out to her:

"Hello! Come here!"

The poor woman heard him call and came back, surprised. She saw Father Martin motioning her to come to him.

"You don't look too well, my beauty." (*My beauty* is an expression often used in old Marseilles. It is used for the fishwives, for the washerwomen, and for all the young and old, poor women working in those parts.)

"I am going to the hospital," the young woman said. "I do hope they will take me with my child. My husband is at sea and I have been expecting him these last three months.''

Just as I am expecting my son, the shoemaker thought.

"He did not come back and now I have no money left and I am ill. So I have to go to hospital.''

"Poor woman!'' the old man said, feeling sorry for her. "No doubt you would like to eat some bread while warming yourself . . . No? . . . Then at least a cup of milk for the little one. Look, here is mine. I have not touched it yet. Get warm and give the little one to me. I had them myself, years ago. I know how to handle them. Yours looks fine. What! You did not give him shoes to wear?''

"I do not have any,'' the poor woman sighed.

"Wait. I have a pair that will fit.''

And with the mother protesting and thanking him, the old workman took the shoes (the ones he had been looking at the night before) and put them on the child's feet. They were a perfect fit.

Martin, however, could not refrain from sighing to himself at parting with his masterpiece. It had been such a treasure to him during his life.

Well, he said to himself, *they are no use to me any more now.* And he went back to the window. He looked so intently that the young woman was surprised.

"What are you looking at?" she asked.

"I am expecting my Master," Martin answered.

The young woman did not understand, or acted as if she did not.

"Do you know the Lord Jesus?" he asked her.

"Certainly," she replied, making the sign of the cross. "It is not so very long ago that I learned my catechism."

"I am waiting for Him," the old man replied.

"And do you think He will pass here?"

"He told me He would."

"Impossible! Oh, how I would love to stay with you to see Him too if that is true — but you must be mistaken. I must be going, in order to be admitted to the hospital."

"Can you read?" the shoemaker asked.

"Yes."

"Well, take this little book," he answered and put a Gospel portion into her hand. "Read it carefully. It will not be the same as seeing Him, but nearly the same and perhaps you will see Him later."

The young woman took the book a little doubtfully. She went away thanking him, and the old man took his place at the window again.

Hour after hour passed; passerby after passerby came and went. The small stove continued to roar and Martin in his chair continued to look at the street.

The Master did not appear.

He had seen a young priest passing by, fair-haired, with blue eyes, just as Christ is shown in the paintings at the church. But just when he went past his house, the priest murmured: "*Mea culpa* [my fault]." Certainly Christ would not have accused Himself like this. It could not be Him.

The young people, the old people, the sailors,

the workmen, the housewives, the great ladies —
all of these passed. Quite a number of beggars
asked the good man for alms; his kind face
seemed to promise something to them. They
were not disappointed.

But the Master did not appear.

His eyes were tired; his heart failed him. The
days are short in December. The shadows had
already lengthened on the square and the lamp-
lighter appeared in the distance. The windows of
the houses opposite began to sparkle joyfully and
the smell of turkey, the traditional dinner of the
Marseilles people, came from all kitchens.

And the Master did not appear.

At last, evening fell and the fog came. It was
therefore useless to stay at the window any
longer. The few passersby who were left dis-
appeared in the fog without anybody being able
to see their faces. The old man went sadly to his
stove and began to prepare his simple supper.

"It was a dream," he murmured. "But still I
did hope."

After finishing his meal, he opened his Book

and wanted to begin reading. But his sadness prevented him from doing so.

"He did not come!" he repeated over and over again.

Suddenly the room was full of a supernatural light and without the door having been opened, the narrow room was full of people. The sweeper was there. The young woman with her child was there — and all said to the old man:

"Didn't you see Me?"

Behind them came the beggars to whom he had given alms, the neighbors to whom he had said a kind word, the children at whom he had smiled. And each one asked in turn:

"Didn't you see Me?"

"But who are you?" the shoemaker said to all of them.

Then the little child in the young woman's arms bent towards the old man's Book and with his finger pointed at the passage where he had opened it:

I was hungry and ye gave Me meat; I was

thirsty and ye gave Me drink; I was a stranger and ye took Me in . . . Inasmuch as ye have done it unto one of the least of these, ye have done it unto Me.

Whosoever receiveth one of these little ones, receiveth Me.

My father had started a watch shop in Amsterdam. He was eighteen years old, and with several friends began a Sunday school. Christmas came, and he and his friends talked over who would give the message at the feast to the children and their parents. It was decided that Father was the one to do that not-too-easy job.

He wrote down the whole talk. That was in the year 1878. I found the booklet in which he had written the message in an old chest in the year 1976 — almost one hundred years later.

3
Casper ten Boom's Christmas Message

FATHER'S CHRISTMAS MESSAGE

If the inhabitants of Bethlehem had known who Joseph and Mary were, and who the little child was who would be born of her — how gladly would they have prepared a little place for Him! But as it was then, it often is today. Many leave the Saviour, who is knocking, standing at the door of their heart, without paying attention to Him. For they have no place for Jesus. Many are too busy with themselves, and do not believe that He is the Son of the living God.

You who are getting on in age — let me ask you, how is it with you? Unto you also is born this day a Saviour, which is Christ the Lord. He came — not in majesty as the King of kings and the Lord of lords — but taking on Himself the form of a servant.

He came, in order that joy would be brought to all the nations, and they would be reconciled with God. He brought peace on earth and wants to bring it also into your soul — that peace which the world cannot give. He is the One who would save His people from their sins.

Do *you* wish to be delivered from your guilt, and be set free from the evil which binds you with chains as a slave?

He calls to you:

I have blotted out, as a thick cloud, thy trans-gressions . . . . though your sins be as scarlet, they shall be as white as snow; though they be red like crimson, they shall be as wool.

Isaiah 44:22; 1:18

Only those who have gotten to know Him as the One who delivered them out of the hands of their enemies, in order to serve Him without fear, in holiness, and justice all the days of their lives — only those who can thank Him for this — are truly free.

For you know: If our Lord were born a thousand times in Bethlehem and not in you, you would be lost anyhow. Oh, for your life's sake, accept His offer — do not send Him away with the answer:

No place for You!

For then you run the risk that when you would wish one day to be allowed to enter the heavenly Jerusalem, the city of the great King, you would be told:

No place for you here!

Then it would be too late for you to cry out, "Oh, if only I had known that!"

It is told that Victoria, the Queen of England, when staying at her summer residence *Balmoral*, likes to take long walks through the woods in simple clothes, and has pleasure in remaining unknown. Some years ago, she was caught in a heavy rainstorm while on one of these trips.

Noticing an old cottage, she ran towards it for refuge. In this cottage lived an old peasant woman alone, who left her house only to take care of her goat and tend her small garden.

The Queen greeted her and kindly asked if she could borrow an umbrella. She added that she would take care to have it returned soon to its owner. The old woman had never seen the Queen, and so she had no idea who she could be.

Therefore she answered in a grudging tone, "Well, I have two umbrellas. One is very good and almost new. I have used it very little. The other one is very worn and has had its time. You may take the old one; the new one I don't lend to anybody — for who knows whether I would ever get it back?" With these words, she gave the Queen the old umbrella, which was torn and battered with spokes sticking out on all sides.

The Queen thought, *With this kind of weather, a bad umbrella is better than nothing at all,* and accepted it politely. Thanking the

woman, she left smiling.

But how great was the horror of the poor old woman, when the next morning, a servant in royal livery entered and returned to her the old umbrella in the name of Queen Victoria — with her thanks — and the assurance that Her Majesty had received good service from it! How sorry she was that she had not offered to the Queen the very best she had, and over and over she cried out, "If only I had known! Oh, if only I would have known!"

This will also be the cry of those who will realize too late who *He* is in the day when all eyes will see Him. Tonight the Saviour comes near to you — not in royal glory — but emptied of it, as a poor little child. And in this humble stature He wants to be received by you. If you have done this, you will one day behold the great King in His beauty.

Then you will also stand in awe and cry out, "I did not know how endlessly great and good You are." For what eye has not seen, nor ear heard, neither have entered into the heart of man, the things which God has prepared for them that love Him.

Have you accepted Him, and can you say with the elderly Simeon about the child in the manger: "My eyes have seen Your salvation, O Lord!"? Then you will also gladly follow the example of the shepherds and widely proclaim the Word which is said concerning this little child. Then the Word of God will receive a place of honor in your family circle.

For if we ourselves have found the greatest treasure, we also want our children to share this privilege with us. Is it not true, parents — you who send your children to our Sunday school — you desire that they will come to know their Saviour at an early age? But you also admit that it takes more than just one hour of Sunday school in the week to attain that purpose.

If you seriously want your child to become a little sheep of the Good Shepherd, you must set an example in your own life. Does the peace of God live in your house and in your heart? Do your children see in you how they must follow the Lord and deny themselves?

A certain father had to inform his son, who was very ill, that he would die soon. The boy answered, "Well, then, I will be with Jesus maybe tonight, Father."

"Yes, my boy," replied the father, and quickly turned around to hide his tears. But the boy, noticing his father's grief, said, "Father, don't weep. When I arrive in heaven, I will immediately go to Jesus and say to Him that as long as I can remember, you have done your best to lead me to Jesus."

Father or mother in our midst tonight: Would your child also be able to speak to you in this way? If not, there may still be an opportunity to repair much. Begin this evening by bowing your knees *with* and *for* your children. The Lord may be found by everyone who seeks Him. If you do this, your way will become like the one of the shepherds, of whom it is written that "they returned, glorifying and praising God."

4
Corrie's Memories
of Christmases Past

Now I am going to tell you how Betsie and I celebrated Christmas in Holland. We worked like a real team and often were the speakers at eight or ten Christmas feasts. In clubs, Sunday schools, hospitals, military groups, and churches — whenever we got a chance.

The Christmas treats were usually the same — Christmas bread with powdered sugar on it and raisins. There was an orange for every child, too. At that time there were no sweet ones in the whole of Holland, and I still remember the sour taste! But it was a joy — a special Christmas joy. Then a cup of hot cocoa. And whenever it was possible, a Christian booklet and a text for the wall with birdies and flowers around a Bible word.

Most of the time we arranged activities in this way: At the first feast Betsie told *the* Christmas story of Luke 2 and I told *a* Christmas story. At the second one we did the opposite — Betsie told *a* story and I *the* story.

In the watchmaking business it was very busy those Christmas days. I can remember that when we went to the feast, tired after a full day, I would count for myself: *"Number four.* Five more evenings — and then we are through Christmas!"

I knew that was wrong and I prayed: *Lord, give me the miracle that I won't get tired but enjoy every Christmas feast, even if it is number ten. Should it not mean joy for everyone that You were born in Bethlehem? So Betsie and I must feel joy to be Your channel.*

God answered that prayer, and all the years we did it, that miracle happened.

Now I want to tell you about a happy and a sad Christmas in my life. Christmas was a feast in our Beje home. Mother and the aunts had a gift for making it as colorful and happy as possible. I remember the holly and the mistletoe — the Christmas table with the red ribbons. Sometimes even a little Christmas tree.

Tante Jans always gave her soldiers a Christ-

mas book and the bookstore sent us a great number from which to choose the best ones. Even as a child I remember the joy of reading through and looking at all those books.

The climax of the feast in the Beje was when we were enjoying Christmas Eve with stories and the singing of carols.

Tante Jans could tell a story so beautifully that nobody could stop listening to her. I remember that the real Christmas event was clearly stressed by her and by Father, who read the Bible from a booklet where you could read not only Luke but also the other Gospels — Matthew 2 following Luke 2, verse 20. All the happenings then followed each other as one great story. Both Father and Tante Jans made it so clear to us that Christmas was for all of us. For *me*. Jesus came for *me*. Jesus was *my* friend, *my* Saviour.

It was Christmas, 1944. Betsie had died. I was in a hospital barracks in Ravensbruck. Dark it was in my heart, and darkness was around me.

There were Christmas trees in the street between the barracks. Why, I don't know. They were the saddest Christmas trees I ever saw in my life. I am sure it was with the purpose of blaspheming that they had thrown dead bodies of prisoners under the Christmas trees.

I tried to talk to the people around me about Christmas, but they mocked, ridiculed, and sneered at whatever I said. At last I was just quiet. It was in the middle of the night that I suddenly heard a child crying and calling, "Mommy! Come to Oelie. Oelie feels so alone." I went to her and saw a child not so young, but feebleminded.

"Oelie, Mommy cannot come, but do you know who is willing to come to you? That is Jesus."

The girl was lying on a bed next to the window, not far from my bed. Although Oelie was completely emaciated from lack of food, she had a sweet face, beautiful eyes, and wavy hair. It was so touching to hear her call for her mother. Oelie had been operated on and the incision on her back was covered by a bandage of toilet paper.

That night I told this poor child about Jesus. How He came into the world as a little baby — how He came to save us from our sins.

"The Lord Jesus loves Oelie and has borne her punishment on the cross. Now Oelie may go to heaven, and Jesus is there right now. He is getting a little house ready for Oelie." Later I asked her what she remembered of what I had told her.

"What is the little house like?" I asked.

"It is very beautiful. There are no wicked people as in Ravensbruck — only good people and angels. And Oelie will see Jesus there."

The child added, "I will ask Jesus to make me brave when I have a pain. I will think of the pain that Jesus suffered to show Oelie the way to heaven." Then Oelie folded her hands; together we gave thanks.

Then I knew why I had to spend this Christmas in Ravensbruck — 1944.

5
The Christmas Story, According to Luke

Chapter 2
Verses 1-20

And it came to pass in those days, that there went out a decree from Caesar Augustus, that all the world should be taxed.

(And this taxing was first made when Cyrenius was governor of Syria.)

And all went to be taxed, every one into his own city.

And Joseph also went up from Galilee, out of the city of Nazareth, into Judaea, unto the city of David, which is called Bethlehem; (because he was of the house and lineage of David:)

To be taxed with Mary his espoused wife, being great with child.

And so it was, that, while they were there, the days were accomplished that she should be delivered.

And she brought forth her firstborn son, and wrapped him in swaddling clothes, and laid him in a manger; because there was no room for them in the inn.

And there were in the same country shepherds abiding in the field, keeping watch over their flock by night.

And, lo, the angel of the Lord came upon them, and the glory of the Lord shone round about them: and they were sore afraid.

And the angel said unto them, Fear not: for, behold, I bring you good tidings of great joy, which shall be to all people.

For unto you is born this day in the city of David a Saviour, which is Christ the Lord.

And this shall be a sign unto you; Ye shall find the babe wrapped in swaddling clothes, lying in a manger.

And suddenly there was with the angel a multitude of the heavenly host praising God, and saying,

Glory to God in the highest, and on earth peace, good will toward men.

And it came to pass, as the angels were gone away from them into heaven, the shepherds said one to another, Let us now go even unto Bethlehem, and see this thing which is come to pass, which the Lord hath made known unto us.

And they came with haste, and found Mary, and Joseph, and the babe lying in a manger.

And when they had seen it, they made known abroad the saying which was told them concerning this child.

And all they that heard it wondered at those things which were told them by the shepherds.

But Mary kept all these things, and pondered them in her heart.

And the shepherds returned, glorifying and praising God for all the things that they had heard and seen, as it was told unto them.